A Freshman's Welcome

but, make sure
you are in loving hands!

Kiriti Sengupta

Edited by Don Martin (Tucson, Arizona)

Hawakaal Publishers

Published by: Bitan Chakraborty, on behalf of **Hawakaal Publishers**, 185, Kali Temple Road, Nimta, Calcutta 700049, India.

First edition: November, 2015

Printed at: Shanti Mudran, Pataldanga Street, Calcutta 700009.

Contact: Bitan Chakraborty (Founder, Hawakaal)

Email: hawakaal.pb@gmail.com

Cell: + 91 9088029197

Cover design: Bitan Chakraborty
ISBN-13: 978-93-85783-63-0
Price: INR Sixty only (Rs. 60/- only)

To

all aspiring Poets

in the World

Thou shalt love thy neighbor as thyself

Introduction

I had no plan to write a chapbook based on personal recollections. I was invited by the publisher, Bitan Chakraborty, to speak at the formal launch of *Heights of Life*, a collection of poems by promising poet Tanmoy Bhattacharjee. Since I had fond memories of the making of the book, I planned to speak on them and wrote a speech accordingly. It came out as a discourse, and Bitan picked it with a definite intention. He advised, "I won't let your effort go in vain!"

The very next day Bitan called me and urged, "Would you mind if I publish your discourse? And if you are okay with my proposal please suggest a suitable title of your work." I felt overwhelmed and spoke with Don Martin, a good friend of mine. We exchanged ideas on the title, and finally we came up with "A Freshman's Welcome."

A Freshman's Welcome is not a marketing tool that can be used to fetch more readers to Tanmoy's book. Rather it portrays the trials and tribulations of an aspiring poet. This book, I think, can boost the zeal of all struggling poets who wish to become published authors.

I have compartmentalized my speech into three chapters here. I believe readers will appreciate and honor my honest views as contained in this book.

Kiriti Sengupta
November, 2015
Calcutta

Tanmoy & I

"I want to buy and read all your books," Tanmoy Bhattacharjee, a young chap from Raiganj, urged in a pleasing tone as we talked for the first time on Facebook Messenger. Did I say Facebook? Did I name a social media? Of course I did. I hope you won't stop reading and listening to me with the very mention of Facebook, for we have a few so-called big names who consider Facebook cheap. They think networking sites are all about poor marketing and fake words of appreciation, especially in the field of literature.

I can remember I inquired, "Do you have enough money to buy all of my books? Do you earn a living?" He assured me that he would buy them all. Eventually he did and I thought Tanmoy belonged to an affluent family. He proved me wrong and told me that he had worked in a private school in the capacity of a teacher, and that the money he spent on my books was all from his hard-earned income. He never claimed a free copy or two, let alone any discount on the selling price. I did not favor Tanmoy with complimentary copies of my books even when he wanted to pass them on to his students and teachers! Little did I know I got an ardent reader who would turn up as an author himself before long.

Tanmoy taught me a lesson although he is almost fifteen years younger than me: Readers have every right to fetch love and blessings from their beloved authors. But, I am not only a poet or an author, I am professionally a teacher who teaches dentistry, and most importantly a hard taskmaster!

A few months back Tanmoy shared his thoughts of publishing his first book of poems and sought my blessings. I turned ruthless and said, "This will just be another book in the market, and poetry has limited readership. Why would you like to publish a book of your own? Is the tag of author so important to you?" He kept silent for a while and replied, "I wish to develop through criticism, and a book will allow me to grow further!" I was pleasantly surprised to say the least, but I turned down his appeal for writing a blurb of his maiden venture under the title *Heights of Life*.

A week later Tanmoy called up with the same request and said, "You may find my poems worthy!" He sounded more confident this time, and I told him to send along the manuscript. He emailed the draft. I promised him that I would get back with my honest remarks on his poetry. Tanmoy's poems looked fresh and clean, although they bore some amount of inhibition attached to them. I called him to say, "When you read poetry aloud you must have a clear throat, and when you write one make sure the ink flows freely from your pen. Poetry has no room for ifs, ands, or buts." Tanmoy followed my suggestions like an obedient student and made a few changes in his poems. Nothing major, but a few punctuation corrections and a couple of word changes were done. The result, I'll say, seemed outstanding! Even then I did not agree to write a blurb for his book, but I managed to write to a few poets and critics for their neutral remarks on Tanmoy's works, and they eventually graced *Heights of Life* with their notes of appreciation.

Tanmoy surfaced again, and this time he met me in person. "I want to get my book published in Calcutta," he pleaded. Among the few publishers I know personally Bitan Chakraborty fitted his bill. I called up Bitan and asked whether he would like to publish a book of poems written in the English language. Bitan readily agreed and assured that he would design the cover himself. In the meantime Tanmoy managed a note from Sudeep Sen, one of the foremost, contemporary Indian English poets. Except for a few technical hindrances Tanmoy's maiden venture was shaped really well under the skilled guidance of Hawakaal Publishers, and I felt happy with the way both the author and the publisher maintained one-to-one contact across the entire length of book publication.

The completed manuscript was being sent to the printer when Tanmoy found one major typographic error on the cover! He quickly informed me and I told him, "Oh well! I thought I did my part satisfactorily, but perhaps you won't allow my exit from the scene until I write a line or two for your book." Tanmoy maintained silence.

I sent along my thoughts to Bitan, and he impressed me with the final cover of the book. Just a one-line blurb that the publisher placed atop on the front cover! It is said, one who writes a blurb is not allowed to write a review of the same book, for a review should read unbiased.

I'm impartial even now. I have seen Tanmoy's growth as a poet, a writer, and certainly as a speaker. He is rapidly evolving, and honestly, it shows. And in a brief span I made him do what I felt right for his development. Sudeep Sen in his short note on *Heights of Life* has written: "... (Tanmoy's) canvas stemming from a small-town upbringing trying to stake an incipient claim on the larger poetic scene." Frankly speaking, I never counted on his upbringing when I offered him a position to speak on my book, *Healing Waters Floating Lamps*, during its formal launch in Oxford Bookstore, Calcutta in April, 2015 although there were eminent dignitaries like Saikat Majumdar, Sharmila Ray, among others! Tanmoy did his job with élan as the moderator in two literary events in Calcutta lately. He has never let me down, and has never made me ponder his so-called "small-town upbringing."

In September 2015 Hawakaal Publishers along with Literature Studio released the expanded second edition of *My Glass of Wine* in Oxford Bookstore, New Delhi. The organizers arranged a writing contest based on "Hybrid Literature." We got a good bunch of submissions across the nation, and both Vibha Malhotra (Founder, Literature Studio) and I chose six writings from the whole lot of entries. Tanmoy was unanimously selected as one of the winners; he ranked fifth among them! All the winning entries were compiled and edited into a chapbook titled *Sankarak* that was published by Hawakaal and it was released on the same date, same place as was *My Glass of Wine*, a best-selling novelette I authored.

Tanmoy's journey from a teacher/postgraduate scholar to a moderately successful creative writer was not an easy affair. It took courage, guts, pain and above all, his never-say-die determination! And now that I am here to release his maiden venture, *Heights of Life*, I'm literally proud of being his beloved author.

Tanmoy & Poetry

I wonder if we welcome a new author or a poet with an open heart! It takes austerities to open the heart, you know. This is very much a part of our primordial Yoga tradition, but then, who cares to listen to the sages of the spiritual capital of this world? My limited understanding of spirituality often leads me to listen to others, especially the new poets who wish to get heard. I was eager to know whether Tanmoy's academic interest and studies have influenced his esthetic and critical consciousness. This was his take on my query:

> Just as a good sense of culture and beauty is not always borne of a standard heritage, similarly the excellent benchmarks of personality like aesthetics, criticality, and creativity do not always come under the purview of any academic discipline. These are all about how one sees and reacts to the world around. I only am grateful for having had the opportunity to study English Literature, the reason of which I came in contacts with some literary scholars who genuinely helped shape my views and values more concrete. All my thoughts and ponderings come directly from the realization of 'Death,' which I found as a predominant theme in many texts there. Arnold's poetry, Sidney's critique, Shakespeare's plays and sonnets, Beckett's 'Godot,' novels by Greene, Wilde, Derrida and Lacan's

theory sincerely turned me mature, at least to the crude reality and acceptance of 'Life.' It might be a worthy but unconscious fact behind the title of my book.

Celebrated Bengali poet Bibhas Roy Chowdhury told me once: "An efficient translator suffers the agony of a surrogate mother." I asked Tanmoy about his stand on poetry and its translation to other languages. His appreciable take is as follows:

> I personally believe that a poet is always a translator. A translator's lookout stems from being a good poet. Literally what a translator does to the poet, a poet, in a similar way, does the same to his thoughts. This is truly the surrogacy of thought.

You can read a full length interview that I held with Tanmoy, published on my blog on September 10, 2015. (Appended to the book)

(https://kiritisengupta.wordpress.com/2015/09/10/miles-to-go/)

Tanmoy has often told me, "Among your other books, I think, *Healing Waters Floating Lamps* (Moments Publication, Ahmedabad) has been an extraordinary work. Very fine, neat and collected!" I was taken aback when I read his review of my book; he has discussed the verses in the light of "Interior Monologue." Although Tanmoy's review of *HWFL* is yet to be published as of today, let me cite his remarks on *Color Code*, a poem that is included in my collection:

> A poet speaks out his "self." A poet speaks out his conditions of subjectivity. A poet speaks out his mind. Also, he expresses right what he is feeling. This is interior monologue. But in dramatic monologue, his subjectivity does not hold any control over his creative mind to obstruct it into creating a form of objectivity. "Nelson Mandela

patch" is not just a poetic usage, nor is this a catchphrase, something Sengupta is truly perturbed with, rather.

Tanmoy has done his homework well enough, I guess. Time will hone his poetic skill, and I'm sure his readers will be happier to witness his growth as a creative writer.

Tanmoy's *Heights of Life*

I had the honor to invite Professor Somdatta Mandal (Department of English & Other European Languages, Visva-Bharati) and Gary Robinson (a poet and writer from Canada) to the formal launch of *Heights of Life* in Santiniketan on 17th of November, 2015. Professor Mandal in her keynote address said:

> As the famous Indian English poet Keki N. Daruwalla had attempted to destroy some myths propagated by some writers, Indian poetry in English is not alien Plant. These poets are not colonialists or neo-colonialists. Also they are not hoity-toity or rich. They are as middle-class as writers in other languages are. Finally they don't have to prove their rootedness in the Indian soil (whatever that may mean), or their nationalism. In his talk at the SAARC Poetry Festival, 2-5 July, 2015, Daruwalla stated: "For twenty years we struggled to tell critics we could write in English as well as others. Then the next twenty went in convincing critics that we   wrote with an Indian sensibility, whatever that is."

> Of course things are different now and Indian poetry in English has changed for the better. We now have many new young poets who write in

English. What these new poets have done is to change the face of Indian poetry in English. They are not averse to run away with reality when they feel like, and mold it to the demands of their poetry. To borrow a phrase from Ranjit Hoskote, their poetic trajectory does not admit to any compass. They avoid heroic or tub-thumping statements, political or social. Language becomes malleable dough in their hands, and they use it with greater aplomb than their predecessors. I am pretty sure that readers will find pleasure in reading the poems of Tanmoy Bhattacharjee, when he states: "I voice the words/Lined up on my tongue/ I try the views I have inherited" while he eagerly awaits with bated breath to gauge the response of his musings.

People, especially my Bengali readers, often ask me why I write in the English language. They think I would have received more appreciation had I written my books in Bengali. I can remember I have addressed this concern in *My Glass of Wine*:

In recent times we are commonly referred to as "Indian English" writers or poets. Honestly speaking, I don't completely concur with this title, and I would like to be known only as an Indian author. In spite of being a developing country, English is no longer a foreign language in India. English is treated as an international language, and is predominantly used in all formal affairs. Moreover, we have here many authors who are regularly writing in English. I don't really know if someone is trying to remind us of our native tongues! Writing in English is no sin, nor is it a lesser offense. This is just a matter of personal choice. What I forgot to write was I would love to be marked as an Indian [Bengali] author. I'm a born

Bengali, and if my writing does not ooze the essence of Bengali culture and traditions I'm only ignoring my being on the earth. Worldwide, Bengalis share a few common interests: spirituality, customs and cuisines, affinity towards *Rabindrasangeet* [songs by Tagore], and sports and politics, among others. Now being a Bengali these will invariably influence my writing, especially the flavor.

Heights of Life, according to me, is a collection of verses written in the English language by a Bengali poet, Tanmoy Bhattacharjee, and I'm not interested to learn if the critics categorize the book under Indian English poetry. My friend and the bestselling author Don Martin (Tucson, Arizona) often refers to my poetry as Bengali poetry although the language is essentially English. I have never asked him why, for I could understand he has emphasized on my native tongue that is Bengali.

Of late I got a chance to speak with two researchers of English literature and they both are familiar with Tanmoy's poetry. I was curious to know their takes on *Heights of Life*. Surprisingly, none of them has used the phrase "Indian English poetry" in their brief notes. Dhritiman Chakraborty who is now working as an Assistant Professor in the English Department of Raiganj Surendranath Mahavidyalaya (Uttar Dinajpur, West Bengal) has opined:

> Tanmoy's poetic-scape is that rare combination where there is the lilting charm of poetic muse speaking to us from its unalloyed ecstasy, it also displays a sensitive mind one who hawks over the contemporary world of simulacra and kitsch. His voice has both the charm of a Virgin Mary and the rage of a fiery Medusa.

And the other researcher, Subashish Bhattacharjee, who is presently a UGC-Research Fellow in the department of English, North Bengal University, has this to say about the book:

> Tanmoy's poems, capturing the essence of the microcosmic imagery, contains the empassioned strain of measuring a tranquil eloquence against my sense of belonging. The poems display a consciousness of one's surroundings that serves to implicate my personal ontological possibilities even as I keep locating roots to realize my beings and becomings as a reader of this poignancy.

As I wrote in the blurb Tanmoy's poems uplift the spirit of the readers. I'll like to place one of his poems here:

I Inquire ... Rain

Music is yours, Rain.
You whisper
We hear
While oneness with earth
You make prosody
Of all the lives within
While you cry
We smile
But when we cry
Where are you, Rain?

Barren lands find meaning
You propel roots and fruits
But who will wash away
The filth of mind?
Let your drops be
Enlivening

What do we expect from poetry? I look out for a secured shelter that will provide some good food for my thoughts. *I Inquire ... Rain* is certainly a readers' delight. Poetry reads best when it treats the philosophies of life in a unique way. Tanmoy writes: "While oneness with earth/ You make prosody/ Of all the lives within/." He has wonderfully projected the interplay of three important constituents of *Panchabhuta*, which is comprised of five classical elements in ancient Hindu scriptures. They are: *kshiti* (soil/earth), *ap* (water), *tej* (fire), *marut* (air), and *byom* (ether/sky). Ancient Greek philosophers believed in them as well. Here Tanmoy uses water (as in rain), earth, and "prosody of all the lives within." It is said rhythm of sound traverses through ether, and it is with the advent of *Omkara*, the sacred sound that refers to 'soul' and is believed to be the ultimate reality of our worldly existence, "the filth of mind" is finally removed. What a poem! Here Tanmoy talks about spiritual communion with poetic allegory by the word "oneness." While in *Mind* Tanmoy reinstates his spiritual quest. He writes:

Mind

I am the mind
Do you know me?
I reside in you
Cry in loss, smile in hope

I am the mind
Do you know me?
I reside in you
I pain, I feel
I love, I leave

I am the mind
Do you know me?
I reside in you
I hide, I heal
I mourn, I kill

17

The Gita urges: Soul can never die, nor it can be destroyed by any means! Soul is immortal. It only takes refuge in the mortal frames, and it is the mind that experiences through our sensory organs like the eyes, ears, nose, tongue and skin. All those "I"s in the poem indicate our "mind" that is the receptor of all our sorrows and delights. Who can forget the wisdom message as rendered by Yogiraj Shyama Charan Lahiree (popularly known as Lahiree Mahasaya)? He had advised: "None is petty, it is the mind which is petty." (Courtesy: *Purana Purusha Yogiraj Sri Shama Churn Lahiree* by Dr. Ashoke Kumar Chatterjee, Yogiraj Publication, Calcutta).

There is no point in citing more examples here. Tanmoy has what it takes to become a great poet. All he needs is practice, and I don't exclude 'spiritual studies' when I say "practice with care!"

Miles to Go

Kiriti Sengupta: Celebrated Bengali poet Bibhas Roy Chowdhury once commented on the work of the translator. He said, "A competent translator suffers the agony of a surrogate mother." What does it take to make a debut as a published author?

Tanmoy Bhattacharjee: I personally believe that a poet is always a translator. A translator's lookout stems from being a good poet. Literally what a translator does to the poet, a poet, in a similar way, does the same to his thoughts. This is truly the surrogacy of thought.

It feels good, without an iota of doubt, to be reckoned as a published author. If everything what is written through pen and paper is a piece of literature, then all human beings are authors. Regarding publishing of an author-piece or being shy is subject to a no-say. To me, it is no different than the feelings of an unable-to-express father to a new-born. It underwent a torrent of stress and strain to make it possible at last. But it was not that easy to make it to the journals, and I was rejected with my poems many a good time. It taught me unuttered that a good profiling is what I need to grace the page of an international journal of well repute. Thereafter, I built my will to approach a publisher, for my individual work. But being a small-town fellow it was hard to find any, In Kolkata. Few people appeared with their tall talks, especially about vanity publishing vs traditional publishing. However, finally Hawakaal Publishers believed in my ideas and approved me of working under their banner. But that was not all. Had my publisher, Shri Bitan Chakraborty not been very kind and tolerant in responding to all my queries, frequent calls of worry, sometimes my 'to be or not to be' stand, then *Heights of Life* would not have been reached to many hands. I would simply opine, in my case, 'justice delayed', but not 'denied'.

Kiriti: Distinguished Indian English poet **Sudeep Sen** has remarked on *Heights of Life*. He has mentioned your "wide-eyed excitement to the world around and within" you. Could you substantiate his observations?

Tanmoy: The syntactical tweaks of his expression seems interesting. Nevertheless, I would say only 'as many men so many minds.' As long as my work is out of my hands, it is wide open to be peeled off. Being a responsible reader and a poet, Mr. Sen has recorded his observation which is true if I have made any justification to Aristotle's dictum, "Know thyself." Anyway, Poetry is a best refuge, I believe so, for those who want to see the unseen and to know the unknown through the 'wide-eyed' lens of a poet.

Kiriti: Worldwide, poetry has a limited market. Aren't you afraid of being cornered as a poet?

Tanmoy: Here I would seek the help of responsible publishers to spread poetry to different quarters of the globe. So that it becomes 'cornered' then too (the new sense in an old bottle). Poetry can never have a short limit. And then, poetry is even greater than poets. Here, I will go gaga over certain issues. It is said that breaking of heart makes a man wise. So do they find shelter in poetry (basically poetry of calf-love). Although a point of debate, whether people opt for poetry just for it is easy to make rhyme, or it does tick their mind and nip easily. T.S. Eliot remarked somewhere that, before 25 we all are poets. But who attempts poetry after that margin, he is really a poet. My point of reference is, poetry should not be generalized. It is not only the weapon of protest, it propagates beauty, reality, love and life too. Publishers should have to step fast to have a good pick. Only lacking in a good circulation, many serious poetry-writers go lost. I am only bothered about the messages that a poet with his poetry conveys. By all means it should go beyond the border of limitation.

Kiriti: Here is a tough task. How would you like to differentiate your poetry from that of other poets of your age?

Tanmoy: I have not yet read all the poets of my age, therefore, I am reluctant to be biased on others' stand. We all want to be different, and this is where we fall all the same. Two words can only be nearest in meaning, not similar. Likewise, ideas might be chanced upon by many heads, but ways of expression will certainly be unlike. My reliance in my poetry grows from the fact that it mirrors my being and having, without any galvanization.

Kiriti: *Heights of Life* is being published by Hawakaal Publishers, Kolkata. How has been your experience working under their banner?

Tanmoy: This is my debut attempt in poetry, and about a publishing house too. Although I think I have served the query well in my very first answer, but again, I can only be assertive of my Publisher (Shri Bitan Chakraborty), who by being cordial and strategic (time to time) helped my reverie in becoming actualized wish. He wanted me to excel at the very first shot. Therefore I placed my plans, and he rectified them, when needed, with his scrupulous consideration. To best express what my poems intend to hint at, we resolved to project few illustrations. One my well-wisher cum friend (Modhura Bandyopadhyay) stepped in the scene with her wondrous paintings, which I must say, truly turned my poems verbose. One thing I ought

21

to mention is, I don't think any publisher would work tirelessly to make the cover page and would go for 4 to 5 times' editing, which Bitan-da did only to make me smile with satisfaction.

Kiriti: Well-known critic and poet Mihir Vatsa thinks his "study of literature as an academic subject" has shaped his "aesthetic plus critical consciousness." You did your Master's in English literature. Do you think the same way?

Tanmoy: Just as a good sense of culture and beauty is not always borne of a standard heritage, similarly the excellent benchmarks of personality like aesthetics, criticality, and creativity do not always come under the purview of any academic discipline. These are all about how one sees and reacts to the world around. I only am grateful for having had the opportunity to study English Literature, the reason of which I came in contacts with some literary scholars who genuinely helped shape my views and values more concrete. All my thoughts and ponderings come directly from the realization of 'death', which I found as a predominant theme in many texts there. Arnold's poetry, Sidney's critique, Shakespeare's plays and sonnets, Beckett's 'Godot', novels by Greene, Wilde, Derrida and Lacan's theory sincerely turned me mature, at least to the crude reality and acceptance of 'Life'. It might be a worthy but unconscious fact behind the title of my book.

Kiriti: You were born and you have been brought up in Raiganj, a small town that is far away from the city lights. Do you think your upbringing has, in any way, influenced your poetry?

Tanmoy: One cannot ignore his root, his origin. So is my stand like. The poems in *Heights of Life* are composed mostly through musing at my study room, in Raiganj. So small-township neither narrowed down my confidence, nor could it strangulate my voice and vision. But, if I differ, in all possible way this is due to my surroundings and its impact.

Anything that accelerates my pen is only my subtle eyeshot. Again, I don't think I would have an extra amount of confidence writing in the lap of city lights.

Kiriti: Name your favorite Indian English poets, and if you could explain your stand.

Tanmoy: Other than the academic perusal (can't help supporting Debjani Chatterjee), I ought to mention the name through whose poetry I understand the charm of lucidity. She is Sharmila Ray. I do desire to read more of her poems, and discover the essence of her poetics. Besides, I find it worth mentioning the poets who represent the Indian panorama well, are Sudeep Sen, Vinita Agarwal, Gopal Lahiri, Vihang. A. Nayak, Sonnet Mondal and of course, Bob D'Costa. But for applying any encomium about the spheres they cling to, I would only resonate my mind – "Miles to go…."

Kiriti: Titir (Titir Banerjee) has been a major inspiration in your literary endeavors, as you have mentioned in the "introduction." Readers would like to know more of Titir and her influences in your life.

Tanmoy: Effort is useless until it forms fruitful action. And I think Titir has come in my life as a catalyst to brush up my dormant dreams. Titir is a postgraduate scholar in English Literature, and is currently working in a school as an Assistant Teacher. She used to be the patient listener of all my scribbling, sometimes hogwash ideas as well. It is she who is my first mentor of poems and poetics. Above all, she believed in me sometimes, when probably I didn't.

Kiriti: Are you an ambitious poet? I would love to hear your dreams and aspirations.

Tanmoy: I don't know how you would name it, but I only want to reach out to more and more people. I fervently believe that I have a message in my poems for all of them; the messages that may serve their want, that may eradicate their afflictions. I aspire to perspire. Nestling in my heart the wish to serve as an inspiring teacher, I just want to keep on working — writing, for myself, for the cause of humanity.